# What Are You Called?

Written by Honey Andersen and Bill Reinholtd
Illustrated by Julian Bruere

A baby dog is called a pup,
but so is a . . .

baby seal.

A baby cow is called a calf,
but so is a . . .

baby elephant.

A baby horse is called a foal, but so is a...

baby donkey.

A baby fox is called a cub, but so is a . . .

baby tiger.

A baby goat is called a kid, and sometimes . . .

we are called kids, too!